Start with SCIENCE

Light

BY
CHARIS MATHER

KidHaven
PUBLISHING

Published in 2024 by
KidHaven Publishing, an Imprint of Greenhaven Publishing, LLC
2544 Clinton St., Buffalo, NY 14224

Written by: Charis Mather
Edited by: William Anthony
Designed by: Drue Rintoul

Photo Credits: Cover – Krakenimages.com, Xaki646, SolidMaks, OsherR, Catur Katamsi, EtiAmmos, wannawit_vck. 4–5 – Hurst Photo, l i g h t p o e t. 6–7 – altanaka, Pushish Images. 8–9 – Eo naya, Natalja Petuhova. 10–11 – manzrussali, Igor Rezende Queiroz. 12–13 – kryzhov, FlyHighMedia. 14–15 – Sunny studio, MichalPrzybylski. 16–17 – IgorZh, irin-k. 18–19 – AndreyUG, WUT. ANUNAI, Suzanne Tucker. 20–21 – Diyana Dimitrova, SUDONG KIM. 22–23 – Alina Demidenko. With thanks to Getty Images, Thinkstock Photo and iStockphoto.

Cataloging-in-Publication Data

Names: Mather, Charis
Title: Light / Charis Mather.
Description: New York : KidHaven Publishing, 2024. | Series: Start with science | Includes glossary and index.
Identifiers: ISBN 9781534544772 (pbk) | ISBN 9781534544789 (library bound) | ISBN 9781534544796 (ebook)
Subjects: LCSH: Light-- Juvenile literature | Optics-- Juvenile literature
Classification: LCC QC360 M38 2024 | DDC 535 --dc23

Manufactured in the United States of America

CPSIA compliance information: Batch #CSKH24: For further information contact Greenhaven Publishing LLC at 1-844-317-7404.

Please visit our website, www.greenhavenpublishing.com.
For a free color catalog of all our high-quality books, call toll free 1-844-317-7404 or fax 1-844-317-7405.

Find us on

Contents

PAGE 4 Think like a Scientist

PAGE 6 Light

PAGE 8 Sources of Light

PAGE 10 Reflection

PAGE 12 Shadows

PAGE 14 Speed of Light

PAGE 16 Plants

PAGE 18 Animals

PAGE 20 In the Real World

PAGE 22 Be a Scientist

PAGE 24 Glossary and Index

Words that look like **this** can be found in the glossary on page 24.

Think LIKE A Scientist

How do we learn about the world? We can ask questions about the different things we see. Scientists are people who find ways to answer questions by doing tests.

Tests help us understand how things work. Some scientists learn about how light works. When scientists learn something new, they write it down so that other people can learn from it too.

Light

We see light every day, but what is it? Light is the thing that helps us to see the world around us. We need light to see, but we cannot touch it.

Without light, everything would be dark. Light can come in different colors and from lots of different places.

Sources of Light

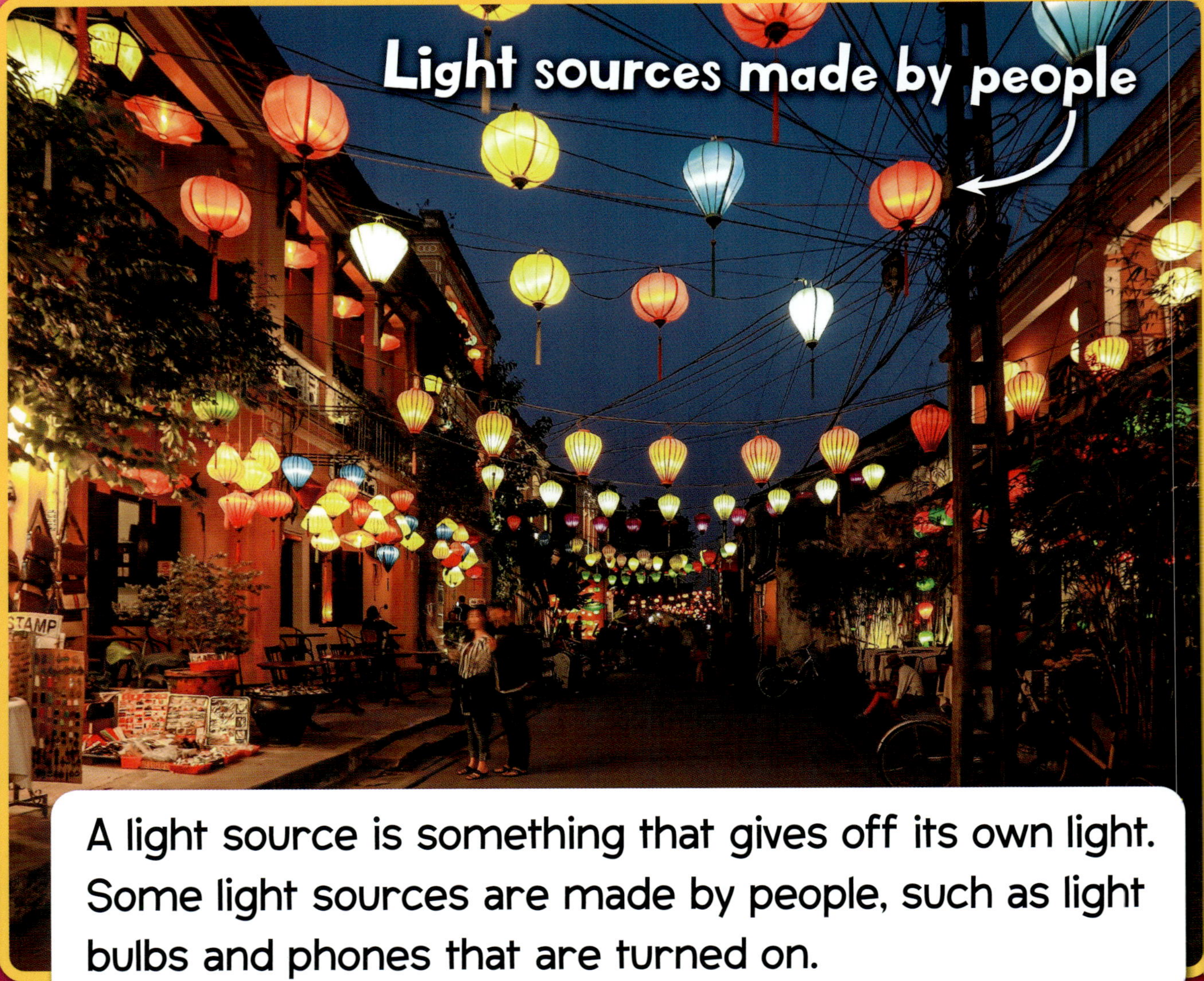

A light source is something that gives off its own light. Some light sources are made by people, such as light bulbs and phones that are turned on.

Some light sources are not made by people. These are called natural sources. The sun is a natural source of light that helps us to see during the day.

Reflection

Things that do not make their own light reflect it. Reflection is when light bounces off something. Our eyes can only see things because of the light coming from sources or bouncing off objects.

Water and mirrors are good reflectors of light.

The moon is not a light source, but it does reflect light from the sun. If we could turn the sun off, we would not be able to see the moon.

Shadows

When objects get in the way of light, they cast dark shadows. Shadows change shape and size when light sources or objects move around.

This person's hands make shadows by blocking the flashlight's light.

Shadows can be long or short. The sunlight makes long shadows in the morning and evening. Shadows are shortest in the middle of the day.

Trees cast long shadows in the morning sunlight.

Speed of Light

There is nothing in the world that travels faster than light. Even sound is not fast enough to keep up with the speed of light.

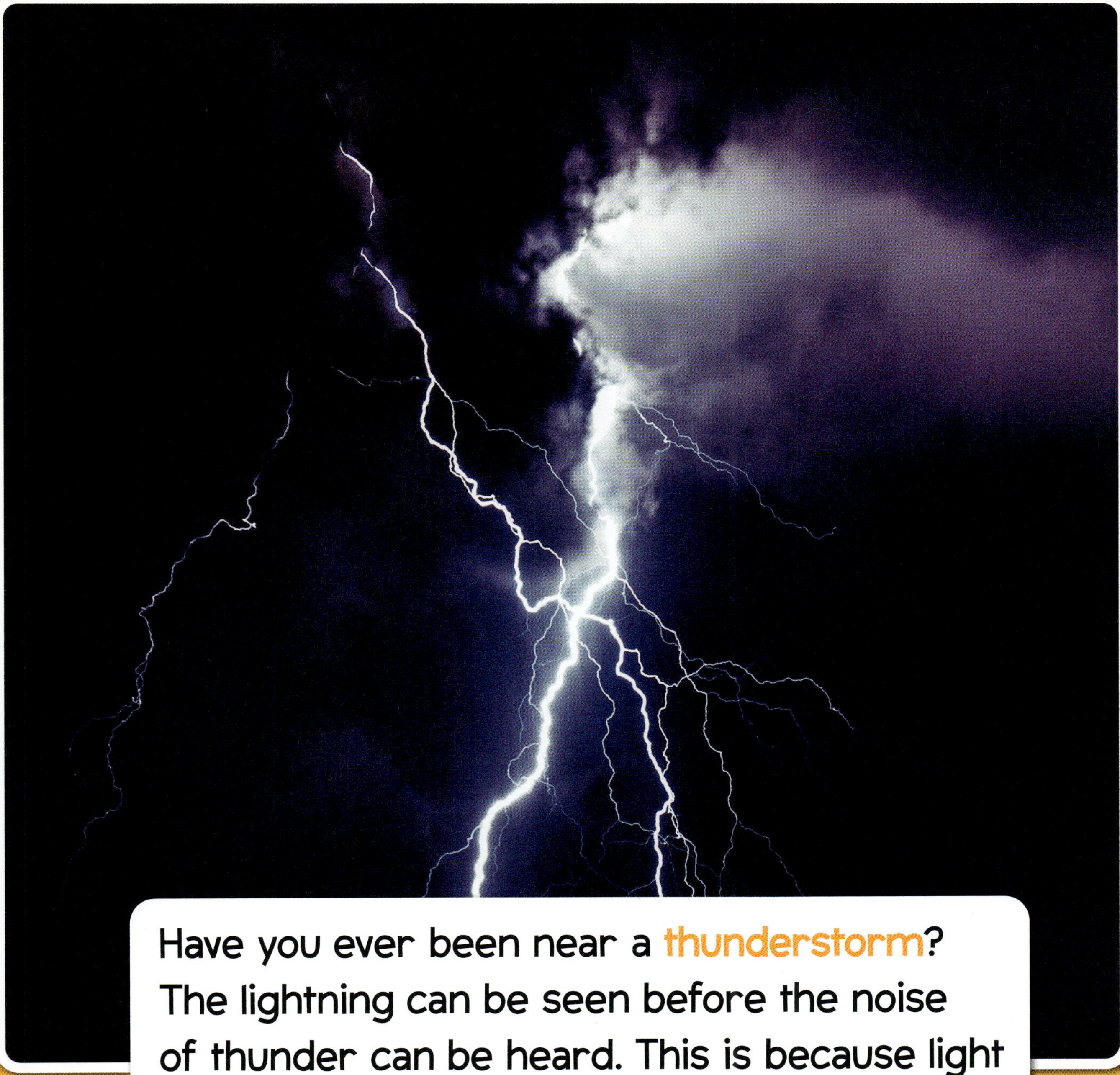

Have you ever been near a thunderstorm? The lightning can be seen before the noise of thunder can be heard. This is because light travels faster than sound.

Plants

Light is very important for life. While we use light to see, plants use it to grow. Plants can turn light into food for themselves. Plants take in light through their leaves.

When light shines on one side of a plant, the plant will grow toward it. Plants next to windows lean toward the sun, which is usually a better light source than indoor lights.

Animals

Some animals can make their own light! Many animals that live in the ocean, such as some types of jellyfish and squid, give off light.

These jellyfish are natural light sources that give off their own light.

There are also some bugs that give off light, such as glowworms and fireflies. Fireflies can light up a part of their body. These bugs use their light to get attention and find a mate.

Fireflies in a forest

IN THE Real World

Light has many uses in everyday life. Sunlight can be very useful for making power. Solar panels collect the sun's light and turn it into **electricity**.

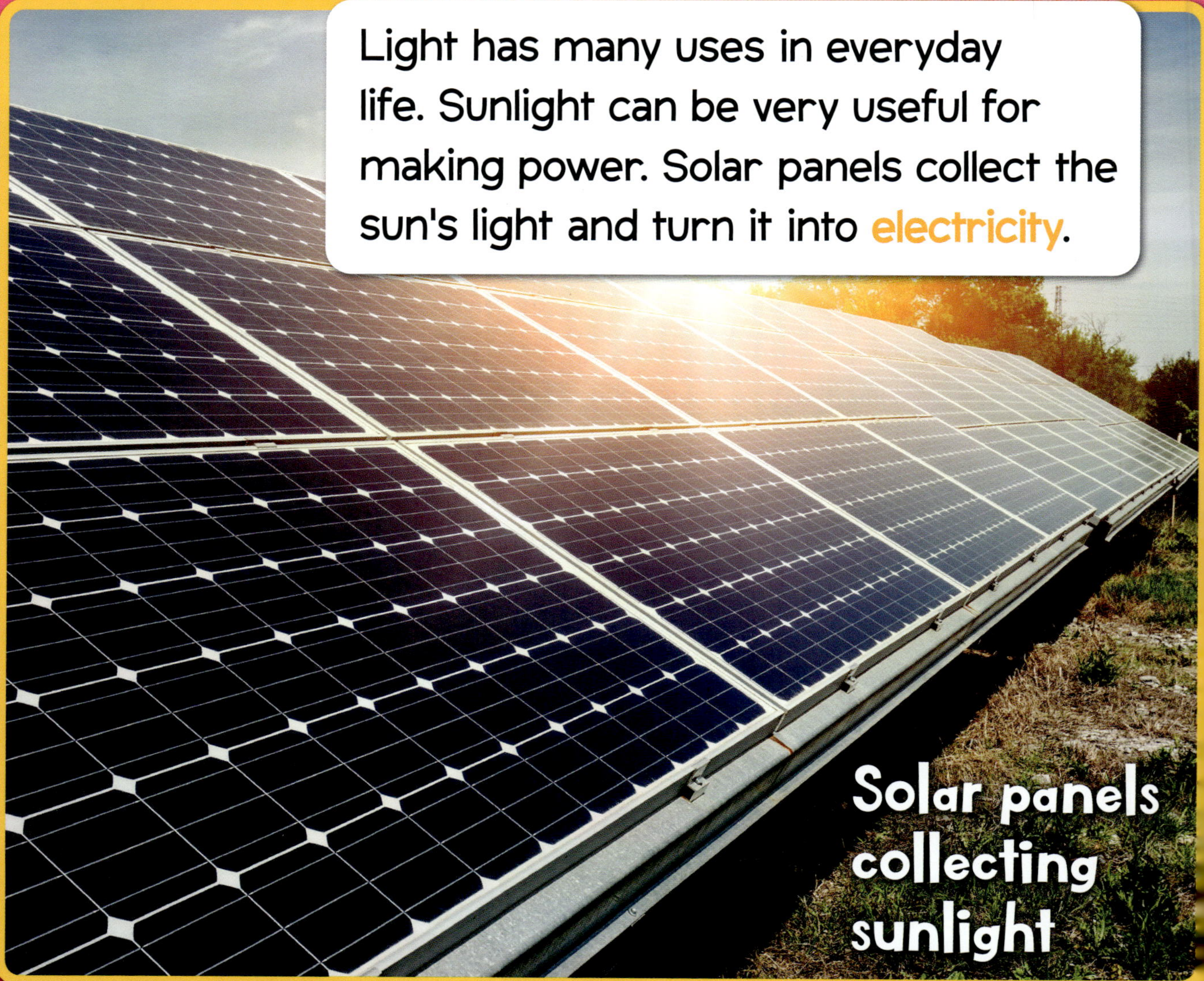

Solar panels collecting sunlight

Light is also useful for drying food. People sometimes dry out tomatoes, grapes, or peppers in the sunlight. Food dried like this will last for a long time and have a strong flavor.

Peppers drying in the sunlight

Be A Scientist

Try your own test with light and shadows. Find a straight stick and a few stones. On a sunny morning, find an open area of grass or sand where you can safely leave your stick.

1. Press your stick into the ground so that it stands up.
2. Mark the end of the stick's shadow with a stone.
3. Come back later in the day to check if the shadow has moved.

What changes did you notice?

Glossary

CAST to stretch over an area

ELECTRICITY energy used to power machines and electronics

MATE a partner, of the same species, that an animal can produce young with

SPEED how fast something moves

THUNDERSTORM a type of storm with strong wind, rain, lightning, and thunder

Index

ANIMALS 18

DARK 7, 12

FOOD 16, 21

MIRRORS 10

MOON, THE 11

PLANTS 16–17

SOURCES 8–12, 17–18

SUN, THE 9, 11, 13, 17, 20–22

WATER 10